25 Two-Minute Talks for CHILDREN
• STORIES THAT TEACH BIBLE TRUTHS •

by Stanley P. Cornils

STANDARD PUBLISHING
Cincinnati, Ohio   2882

DEDICATION

This book is dedicated
to
Kristie and Kevin Cornils,
two of my grandchildren
who helped me write it,
to a host of children in the congregations
where I have ministered and shared these stories,
and to the many friends who encouraged
me to put them into print.

Unless otherwise indicated, all Scripture quotations are taken from the HOLY BIBLE: NEW INTERNATIONAL VERSION, Copyright, © 1973, 1978 by the International Bible Society. Used by permission of Zondervan Bible Publishers.

Sharing the thoughts of his own heart, the author may express views that are not entirely consistent with those of the publisher.

ISBN 0-87239-867-6

Copyright © 1985 by Stanley P. Cornils, Vallejo, California. Published by the STANDARD PUBLISHING Company, Cincinnati, Ohio. A division of STANDEX INTERNATIONAL Corporation. Printed in U.S.A.

CONTENTS

Introduction	5
I Forgot to Tell You	7
The Legend of the Dogwood	8
The Holiday That Is Different	9
The Cobbler and His Guest	11
Monkey Business	14
Destiny in a Box of Rubbish	15
The Butterfly That Never Flew	17
Garbage in the Salad	19
Nail Soup	20
How Much Do You See?	22
Sin Will Drag You Down	23
Johnny Appleseed	24
Bad Company	26
Processional Caterpillars	28
Will Wishing Make It So?	30
The Little Boat Twice Owned	31
A Feathered Tale	33
How Hercules Killed the Monster	35
Using the Pieces	36
No Magic Faucets	38
The Irritated Oyster	40
Don't Sell Your Wings	41
The Importance of Little Things	43
Chocolate Cake	45
Good Work Pays Off	46

INTRODUCTION

"Tell me a story" is a request almost as old as childhood itself. Few of us ever outgrow our alacrity to listen. When a story teaches a moral or spiritual truth, its value is enhanced because it then becomes a teaching tool. The Jewish Talmud is an excellent example of the use of stories to pass on ethical and religious precepts.

This collection of stories is intended for the use of ministers, Sunday-school teachers, junior church leaders, Vacation Bible School workers, teachers in Christian schools, Bible Club leaders, parents, and anyone else who ministers to the spiritual needs of children.

In most of my fifty years as a pastor, I have reserved at least five minutes of the morning worship service for a message especially for children. That message consisted either of a story or an object lesson.

Only a small percentage of these stories are original with me. As for the others, in many instances the sources have been lost or were never known. Some of them have been a part of our culture for generations and are common property, but deserve to be told again. In no instance have I knowingly copied another's composition without giving credit.

In the telling of some of them, I have not accented the moral or spiritual truth because it is obvious. I would suggest that you make your own application and elaborate as the age and understanding of your audience dictates. Tell it in your own way and words and memorize only the sequence and the fundamental details.

Jesus took time to minister to children; may He bless you as you follow in His footsteps.

Stanley Cornils

I FORGOT TO TELL YOU

It was during the week before Easter. The streets and stores were filled with people buying something new to wear on Easter Sunday. A little boy stood gazing into a store window. In that window was displayed a huge painting showing the crucifixion of Jesus. Three crosses stood on top of a hill, each with a lifeless man upon it. Roman soldiers and other people were standing around. The boy seemed to be in deep thought as he studied the scene.

A man walking by noticed the boy. He slowed his pace, approached the window, and stood silently beside the lad. "That's Jesus in the middle," the boy explained. "They killed Him—and He never hurt anyone. Those fellows with the spears and shields are the Roman soldiers. They had to carry out the crucifixion. And most of the other people are Jews. They hated Him; they lied about Him and persuaded the Roman governor to crucify Him. And He never did anybody wrong.

"After He died, everybody went home, and some of His friends took His body down and put it in a tomb."

As the boy finished his explanation, the man walked away thoughtfully. After a few seconds, the boy ran after him, shouting, "Hey, Mister! Wait! I forgot to tell you something." The man slowed his walk as the boy neared. "I forgot to tell you the most important part: He didn't stay dead. He rose on Easter Sunday, and He's alive and with God in Heaven today."

Let's not forget the most important part of Easter. Jesus is alive!

THE LEGEND OF THE DOGWOOD

The dogwood tree is a small, twisted tree with cross-shaped blossoms. Years ago, someone made up this story about how it got to be that way.

Long, long ago, the dogwood used to grow big and strong, like the oak and other forest trees. So strong and firm was its wood that it was chosen for the timber for Jesus' cross. Being used for such a cruel purpose made the tree very sad. Jesus knew this; so He smiled on it and said,

"Because of your sadness for my suffering, I make you this promise: Never again shall the dogwood tree grow large enough to be used for a cross. Henceforth, it shall be slender and bent and twisted. Its blossoms shall be in the form of a cross—two long petals and two short petals. In the center of the outer edge of each petal there will be nail prints, brown with rust and stained with blood. In the center of the flower there will be an image of the crown of thorns, and all who see it will remember that it was upon a dogwood tree I was crucified, and this tree shall not be mutilated or destroyed, but cherished as a reminder of my death upon the cross."

Like the dogwood tree in this story, we are sad about the cruel way Jesus died. But we are glad to know He died for us.

THE HOLIDAY THAT IS DIFFERENT

"Give thanks in all circumstances" (1 Thessalonians 5:18). "Praise the Lord, O my soul ... and forget not all his benefits" (Psalm 103:1, 2).

Thanksgiving Day is different from all the other special days we celebrate. There is no holiday quite like it in our calendar. It does not celebrate the winning of a battle, or the founding of a nation, or the birth of any great person, nor any political or social revolution. On Thanksgiving Day, we are not celebrating George Washington, or Columbus, or the freeing of the slaves, or the Declaration of Independence, but just the fact that a wonderful and loving Heavenly Father provides so bountifully for us.

The first American Thanksgiving Day took place in the fall of 1621, about a year after the Pilgrims landed on this continent. That first year in the new world was a difficult one for the Pilgrims. One hundred two people landed at Plymouth Rock in 1620. During the winter that followed, forty-seven of them died. Just being able to keep alive was a real struggle. They had many reasons for being afraid. Behind them lay 3000 miles of the Atlantic Ocean; ahead of them, miles and miles of wilderness filled with wild animals and unfriendly Indians.

Because the Pilgrims were religious people, they often took their troubles to God in days of fasting and praying. But it seemed that always thinking about their troubles made them gloomy and discontented. In some, it even created the desire to go back to the old world from which they had so recently come, even with its religious persecution.

One historian tells us that late in the year 1621, one of the colonists suggested that they set aside another day for fasting and praying. However, one of their number, an older man with a great deal of wisdom and common sense, arose in the meeting and said he thought they should consider their blessings instead.

"After all," he said, "the colony is growing strong, the fields have produced a good harvest, there are plenty of fish in the rivers and plenty of game in the forests, and the climate is very healthy. Our wives are beautiful and our children are well behaved. Finally, we have what we came for—full civil and religious liberty. I would amend the resolution for a day of fasting and prayer and propose instead that we have a day of giving thanks to God for the many blessings which are ours." The idea seemed good to the people and they decided to take his suggestion. That is how the first Thanksgiving Day came about.

A couple of years later, the land was dry and in need of rain, and another day of fasting and praying was set. But that day was changed to a thanksgiving celebration when it began to rain during the prayers. Gradually, more and more of the governors in the New England colonies began to proclaim a day of Thanksgiving each year following harvest. The custom of having a Thanksgiving celebration spread through many other states by the middle of the nineteenth century. In 1863, President Lincoln appointed a national day of Thanksgiving, the last Thursday of November. In 1941, Congress made the fourth Thursday of November the official Thanksgiving Day.

Someone has said that gratitude is the memory of the heart. Our word *thanksgiving* comes from an Anglo-Saxon word which means "to think." In the German language there is the word *denken,* which means "to think." They have another word, *danken,* which means "to thank." You see, the two words come from the same root. Thinking and thanking always go together.

If we would just think of all the blessings we have, of how much we owe to God and others, and how much we depend on them for what we have to enjoy, we would be thankful. Counting blessings is good arithmetic.

Those earliest colonists of our country did not set a day for thanksgiving because everything in their new world was going right, but they set a good example of giving thanks in all circumstances (1 Thessalonians 5:18). After all, God doesn't wait until the fourth Thursday in November to bless us—so why should we wait until then to thank Him? If we are thinkful, we will be thankful. "Give thanks in all circumstances.... Praise the Lord ... and forget not all his benefits."

THE COBBLER AND HIS GUEST

Many years ago, there lived an elderly shoemaker. He was a kind and generous man who lived all alone in the city of Marseille, in southern France. Everyone who knew him loved him, because he always seemed to be looking after the needs of other people. He was known as Father Martin.

One Christmas Eve, as the story goes, he sat alone in his shop reading the story of the first Christmas from his Bible. He was particularly fond of the story of the Wise-men, who came from far away countries to see the baby Jesus and to bring their gifts of gold, frankincense, and myrrh. After he had finished reading, he closed his Bible and said to himself: "If this were the first Christmas, and Jesus were to be born in Marseille, I know just what gift I would give him." He arose from his chair, walked over to the shelves that lined his shop, and took down a pair of tiny, soft, white leather shoes with silver buckles. "These are the finest shoes I have ever made," he said to himself. "I'm sure His mother would be glad for Him to have them. But I'm just a silly and sentimental old man, dreaming of things that could never happen. Besides, the Lord has no need of any poor gift from me."

He walked back to the shelf, replaced the shoes, blew out the flickering candle, and went to bed. It all happened so soon after his retiring that he didn't know whether he was asleep and dreaming, or whether he actually did hear the Lord calling him by name.

"Martin, you have loved me for many years. You have always wanted to see me. Tomorrow I will walk by your shop. If you see me and invite me in, I will be your guest and will sit with you at your table."

For most of the night, Martin hardly slept at all. He was too filled with joy. Long before the sun came up, he was out of bed, tidying up his quaint little shop. Whatever happened that night seemed so real to him that he actually believed that the Lord talked with him and that He really was going to visit him that day. After he had cleaned the scraps of leather from the floor and freshly dusted everything in the shop, he decorated the rafters with some fresh, green fir boughs. On his table he placed a loaf of bread, a pot of honey, a pitcher of milk, and a few other things that would become part of a wholesome meal. Over the fire there hung a pot of freshly made coffee. If you had come in about that time, you would have known that Martin was eagerly expecting company.

In Marseille, as in many cities and countries of the world, Christmas is a holiday. Instead of working at his bench making and mending shoes, Martin spent all day just looking out of his window. He was sure that if the Lord were to come down his street, he would recognize Him. The day was dreary and bitterly cold, with rain and driving sleet. The street was almost deserted. This did not discourage Martin. All he could think about was the joy that would be his when he would sit down with his Lord at his humble table.

As he sat at his window waiting for his Guest to arrive, an old street-sweeper walked by. He was blowing his breath upon his thin, gnarled hands, trying to keep them warm. Martin thought, "Poor man, he must be half-frozen." Quickly he opened the door and called to him, "Come into my shop, warm yourself by my fire, and have a cup of hot coffee." Of course, the man accepted his invitation, and Martin shared his hospitality with him.

A bit later, Martin noticed a sickly and thin lady carrying a baby. She was poorly clothed for such cold weather. She looked so weak and ill, as though she might not be able to take another step. As she stopped for a few moments to rest in the shelter of his doorway, Martin opened the door. "Come in and rest in my shop and warm yourself by my fire." Looking at her carefully and tenderly, he asked, "Are you not well?"

"I am on my way to the hospital. I don't know whether they will take me and my baby in. I have no money. My husband is away at sea, and I have no one to whom I can go," she explained.

"Poor child," he said, "you must have something to eat while you are getting warm. I'll heat a cup of milk for the little one. Ah, what a bright-looking little boy he is. But he has no shoes on his feet."

"He has no shoes," sobbed the mother.

"Well, I can soon take care of that," said Martin. He walked to the shelf and took down the little snow-white shoes with the silver buckles. He put them on the baby's feet—they fit perfectly.

After the woman and her baby had eaten, she thanked Martin graciously and prepared to leave. The old man pressed a few coins into her hand and helped her to the door. Then Martin went back to his place at the window.

The day went by ever so slowly. Through the day, many needy folk had shared in Martin's hospitality, but his expected Guest had not arrived. At nightfall, Martin lay down on his cot with a heavy and disappointed heart. He said to himself, "Maybe it was only a dream. I did hope and believe. I prepared for His coming, but He did not come."

Martin was just dropping off to sleep when suddenly the room was filled with a glorious light. Was it a dream? Was it real? Martin didn't know, but there appeared to his astonished eyes the street-sweeper, the sick mother and her baby, and all the other people he had befriended in his shop that day. As they passed by, each one smiled and said, "Did you not see me? I warmed myself at your fire today and ate from your table."

Then, just like the night before, he heard the gentle voice of the Master, repeating the familiar words: "Whatever you did for one of the least of these brothers of mine, you did for me" (Matthew 25:40).

MONKEY BUSINESS

"A gentle answer turns away wrath, but a harsh word stirs up anger" (Proverbs 15:1).

We cannot always choose what we will meet as we go through life, but whatever it is, we have to decide what we will do about it. It would be nice if we only met with happy things. But we don't. Sometimes people are mean or angry with us, and they say unkind things. This story reminds us that if we meet angry words with angry words, the result will be more angry words. But if we're nice, we can cool off the anger.

Jocko was a tiny monkey who belonged to and travelled with an organ-grinder. One day they were making their way down a city street with Jocko in the lead. He was holding out his tin cup to receive the offerings of the people who heard the organ-grinder's music.

Suddenly a large dog spied Jocko, and you don't even have to guess at what happened. The dog ran barking, growling, and prancing toward the colorfully dressed little creature standing on the sidewalk. People stopped to see what would happen. Jocko stood perfectly still, waiting for the dog to arrive. Now, that in itself is enough to confuse anyone, for when a dog wants to chase something, he expects it to turn tail and run for its life.

But instead of running, the monkey stood still. Just when the dog was a few steps away, Jocko courteously bowed and tipped his hat. The dog froze in his tracks, and the bystanders laughed at his embarrassing and baffling situation. He stood motionless for a few moments, probably wondering what to do next. Things just weren't working out as he had planned. Soon his head drooped, his tail dropped between his legs, and he walked away.

As for Jocko, he jumped up on his master's organ, and peacefully they moved on down the street. It was clear that this monkey wanted no disagreements. Somewhere he had learned that it takes two to start a quarrel, and one to stop it.

If you have never tried this kind of self-defense, I'd suggest that sometime you put it to the test. You might be in for a surprise!

DESTINY IN A BOX OF RUBBISH

"He that is faithful in that which is least is faithful also in much" (Luke 16:10, KJV).

Every now and then the "Boy Wanted" sign went up in the window of Peters Hardware store. Mr. Peters was a wealthy man, but many people thought he was a bit strange. Boys were always applying for the job. It was easy work and the pay was sure, but none of the boys lasted long on the job.

Maybe the reason was that Mr. Peters was really looking for more than just a boy to run errands. Frank Adams found that out the day he went to work for Mr. Peters. The morning went fast because the boy was busy. About the middle of the afternoon, Mr. Peters asked him to go up to the attic. There he would find a long wooden box filled with all kinds of things. He was to put it in order.

What did he find? Old rusty nails, screws of all sizes, washers, bolts, nuts, keys, nails—rubbish. The wind blew through the cracks in the wall, mice scurried about the place, and cobwebs were everywhere.

"If Mr. Peters thinks I'm going to stay up here and rummage through this junk, he's mistaken," Frank said to himself as he closed the door to the room and went down the stairs.

"Have you put it all in order already?" inquired Mr. Peters.

"No, I didn't find anything worth putting in order; besides, I thought I was hired to run errands," Frank replied.

"Oh," said Mr. Peters, "I thought you were hired to do as you were told," but he smiled pleasantly as he said it; so nothing more was made of it. At six o'clock, Mr. Peters called Frank and paid him the amount they had agreed upon for a day's wages. He then informed him that his services were no longer needed.

The next morning, the "Boy Wanted" sign was in the window again. Before noon, Sammy Pittman had applied and was accepted as the errand boy. He was busy all day. Just an hour before closing time, he became acquainted with the big box in the attic and was instructed to put it in order. He wasn't afraid of the cold, or mice, or cobwebs, but he couldn't see any good reason for spending much time on the contents of the box. He grumbled to himself as he tumbled the articles around. He picked out a few of the better-looking items and reported back to Mr. Peters. "These are about the only things worth keeping," he said as he handed them to his employer. By the end of the day, he too had been told that he did not need to return, and the sign went back in the window.

Willard Smith was the next boy to get the job. He did not learn of the big box until the morning of the second day when he was sent to put it in order. He worked all morning until Mr. Peters called up, "Got through?"

"Oh, no! There's ever so much more to do," he replied.

"Come on down now and you can finish it after lunch," Mr. Peters suggested.

All that afternoon he worked quietly over the contents of the box; it wasn't until almost closing time that he reported back to his employer. "I've done the best I could," he said. "At the bottom of the box I found this five-dollar gold piece." He handed it to his employer.

"That's a funny place for a gold piece; well, I'll see you in the morning," Mr. Peters said as he dropped it into his pocket.

Later that evening, Mr. Peters went to inspect the finished task. There lay the long, deep box into which rubbish from the sweepings of the floor had been dumped for many years—now all in order. Willard had fitted wooden shingles together and made compartments for the different items and labeled each one: "Good screws, Washers, Bolts, Nuts, Picture nails," and more. As he inspected the boy's work, Mr. Peters said to himself, "I think I have found me a boy. And he has found a fortune."

The sign was never seen in the window again. Willard Smith became the well-known errand boy of Peters and Company. Shortly after going to work for him, Mr. Peters presented him with a motto that read, "He that is faithful in that which is least, is faithful also in much," with the suggestion that he hang it on the wall of his bedroom. Mr. Peters explained that the motto "tells your fortune—don't forget it."

This all happened many years ago, and Willard Smith is no longer an errand boy, but a part of the firm of Peters, Smith, and Company. Through faithfulness in small things, he found his fortune in a box of rubbish.

THE BUTTERFLY THAT NEVER FLEW

"Consider it pure joy ... whenever you face trials of many kinds, because you know that the testing of your faith develops perseverance ... so that you may be mature and complete, not lacking anything" (James 1:2-4).

One day while playing in the orchard, Tommy noticed a cocoon on one of the low-hanging branches. He picked it off and took it to his house. As he held it in his hand, he could feel movement inside, a sort of thumping or kicking as though something were trying to get out.

When his father came home that evening, Tommy showed him the cocoon. His dad said sometime last fall a worm, or caterpillar, had crawled onto the limb. In order to prepare itself for winter, it spun the threads of the cocoon and made itself a shelter from the harsh weather of winter. Now that spring was here, it was time for it to be born into another form. But in order for that to happen, it had to work its way out of its prison.

The next morning as Tommy thought about it and felt the movement inside, he felt sorry for whatever it was that was trying to kick its way out. He wanted to help release it; so he carefully began to unwind the threads of the cocoon—yards and yards of it lay on the floor as he carefully worked with it. Finally it was finished, and Tommy held in his hand a brand new butterfly. And to think—he had helped it to be born! He felt proud for having released it from its prison. He took it outdoors so it could dry in the warm sun. How beautiful it was as it opened its wings, but he noticed that it made no effort to fly. He was afraid something was wrong, and it was. Before the day ended, the butterfly had died.

Tommy asked his father why his butterfly had died. His dad said, "The butterfly's struggle to free itself from the cocoon is a necessary part of the development of its muscles—especially those of the wings. If it doesn't get that exercise, it can't survive."

Tommy was very sad. He had meant to help, but in robbing the butterfly of its struggle, he had deprived it of a necessary part of its growth.

While we are growing up and even after we become adults, we often grow impatient when we have to struggle with trials and troubles. It has always been that way. In our Bible verse for today, James reminds us that "trials (struggles) develop perseverance ... so that you may be mature and complete." That big word "perseverance" means the ability to keep going, being firm, having backbone.

If you were to run 100 feet each day for a week, then 200 feet each day the next week, and keep increasing the distance each week, soon you would be able to run a whole mile without stopping. If you continued the struggle by increasing the distance every few days, you would eventually be able to run five, ten, fifteen miles and finally the marathon, which is over twenty-six miles.

Most people do not enjoy having to struggle this hard for anything. The writer of Hebrews said it this way: "Endure hardship as discipline.... No discipline seems pleasant at the time, but painful. Later on, however, it produces a harvest of righteousness and peace for those who have been trained by it" (Hebrews 12:7, 11).

People with well-developed muscles strengthened and increased them by strenuous exercise. There is no other way. We grow strong by struggling. It is true in the physical world, and it is true in the spiritual world. If everything in life were to come easily, our strength would not properly develop. And our characters, instead of being strong, would be flabby and frail.

GARBAGE IN THE SALAD

One day a mother was working in the kitchen, scraping, peeling, and cutting vegetables for a salad. Her daughter came to ask permission to attend a certain movie with some of her friends from school. Because it was not the sort of movie a good girl should see, the mother explained her reasons and did not grant the permission. The daughter admitted that the movie did have a bad rating, and probably was questionable, but she insisted that all the other girls were going and none of them thought it would harm them.

As she continued to argue and plead and put on a scene, she saw her mother suddenly pick up a handful of vegetable scraps, peelings, and unsightly pieces and toss them into the salad. In a startled voice the girl cried, "Mother, you're putting the garbage in the salad."

"Yes," replied her mother, "I know I put the garbage in the salad, but if you thought it was all right to put garbage in your mind and heart, you certainly wouldn't mind a little in your stomach."

Very thoughtfully and carefully the girl removed the garbage from the salad. Then, with a short, but sincere apology to her mother, she went to inform her friends that she would not be going with them.

Sometimes we think our parents say no too often. We want to have fun with our friends, and it seems our parents want us not to have fun. But Christian parents are trying to help their children. They want the children to have fun, but in good, safe ways. They don't want "garbage" in their children's lives any more than they want garbage in their children's food.

NAIL SOUP

One day near nightfall, a tramp was walking through the forest, very much afraid that he would not find shelter before darkness overtook him. Suddenly he saw a light between the trees. Heading in that direction, he soon came to a little house and gently knocked on the door. An elderly little lady opened the door and very sternly inquired of him: "What is your business here?"

"I would like shelter for the night and something to eat," he responded.

"I haven't a bite in the house," she said. "I am alone and my house is not an inn; you will have to go elsewhere."

After much pleading on his part, she finally permitted him to enter and offered him a place on the floor where he might sleep for the night. In looking around the room, it appeared to him that she was not as poor as she had led him to believe. So again he asked her for some food.

"I haven't a thing to eat in the house," she said. "I haven't had a bite to eat all day."

Being a cunning and crafty knight of the road, he said, "Well, then, I shall have to ask you to eat with me."

"Eat with you?" she exclaimed. "You don't have anything to eat."

"I shall show you," said the man. "Would you please loan me one of your stew pots?" Quickly she brought one from the cupboard. He filled it with water and placed it on the kitchen stove. When the water began to boil, he took a nail from his pocket and dropped it into the pot.

"Just what is that going to be?" she asked.

"Nail soup," he replied as he began to stir the water.

"Nail soup?" she asked. "I have never heard of such a thing."

"Watch me," said the tramp as he continued to stir. "A nail makes excellent soup, except that this might be pretty thin because I've been using this same nail for a whole week now. If I just had a little bit of flour, I'm sure that would help."

"I think I have some flour," she said as she brought a cupful to him.

He poured it into the pot and went on stirring. Soon he broke the silence, "Now if I had a small piece of beef and a few potatoes, we could have soup that would be fit for the king's table."

"I think I could find a few potatoes and a bit of beef. Here, put them in the soup," she said as she handed them to him.

"Miracle of miracles!" she said, as she admiringly watched him. "And all with a nail."

As he continued to stir, he made one more suggestion, "A pat of butter, a bit of milk, and salt and pepper would finish it off just right."

"I have some butter," she answered, "and my cow provides plenty of milk." She brought the butter and milk and salt and pepper, which he ceremoniously added to the contents of the pot as he continued stirring. After a few minutes, he pulled the nail out of the mixture, took a small sip of the soup, and proudly announced that it was ready to eat. She was so pleased that she also provided bread, butter, cheese, and a cake, and the two of them sat down and enjoyed a tasty meal.

She was so fascinated with him that she gave him a bed for the night, fed him breakfast in the morning, and even handed him some money, saying, "Thank you for what you have taught me. Now I shall never go hungry because you have taught me how to make soup with a nail."

"Well, it really isn't hard," he said, "so long as you have some good things to put into it."

As she watched him go on his journey, she said to herself, "Such people don't come this way every day."

Of course, this story is only a folk tale—sort of a joke. But it has a real meaning for us! You can get something good out of life if you put something good into it, like studying, trying, and doing good things for others. The result will be in direct proportion to what you have put in.

HOW MUCH DO YOU SEE?

The name of Marshall Field is familiar to a great many people. Many years ago, this man started what later became the largest department store in Chicago. The story is told that one day two country boys, who were friends, came to Mr. Field and applied for jobs in his store. Both of them were hired to do chores around the store.

As time passed, one of the boys was promoted to a more responsible and better-paying position. His friend, who was not promoted, was so shaken by this that he went to Mr. Field and complained. He felt that he had worked hard and conscientiously, and that he also deserved a promotion.

Mr. Field listened attentively and respectfully to his story. Then he said, "Yes, you have worked hard and faithfully. I hear noises in the alley; would you please go down there and see what is going on?"

In a matter of minutes the boy returned and said to Mr. Field, "There is a big truck down there loading goods."

"Fine," said Mr. Field, "Now go and see what kind of goods they are loading."

Soon the boy returned and reported, "They are loading cases of gloves."

"That's fine," said his employer. "Now go and find out where the gloves are being sent."

Soon the boy returned and reported, "To Dubuque, Iowa, Sir."

"You stay right here," said Mr. Field, "and I will call your friend." When his friend arrived, Mr. Field said exactly the same thing to him: "I hear noises in the alley; would you please go down there and see what is going on?"

In a very short time the boy returned and reported, "There is a big truck loading cases of gloves, which are being shipped to Dubuque, Iowa, Sir."

Then Mr. Field addressed the complaining lad, "It took you three trips to the alley to find out what your friend discovered in just one trip. I hope you understand why he got the promotion instead of you. Use your eyes."

SIN WILL DRAG YOU DOWN

One day a great eagle was soaring in circles over a lake, apparently looking for food. All at once, he aimed his body almost straight downward toward the surface of the lake. When he hit, there was a spray of water, followed by much splashing of fins and feathers. Ultimately, it seemed that the eagle had won the battle as he began to rise to the sky with a two-foot fish clutched in his claws. Slowly he rose in the air with the fish dangling and wriggling, trying to get free. But when the eagle reached a height of about a thousand feet, he began to fall. He gained speed as he fell until he landed with a great splash in the water. Later someone found the bird and the fish—still together, both dead.

The eagle's claws are long, curved, and very sharp. When he grabs an animal or fish, his claws sink deeply into the victim's body. Apparently the eagle had found the fish too heavy to carry. But he could not release it because his claws were so tightly and deeply sunk into the flesh of the fish. No matter what movements the eagle made, he could not free himself.

The same sort of thing often happens to people. The things we want and think we can control (the kind of friends we have, the habits we develop, the goals we strive for) may eventually overpower us and pull us down spiritually. What once seemed to be a small and manageable influence in our lives turns out to be so big and strong that it eventually imprisons us. We may be, like the eagle, powerless to set ourselves free. But unlike the eagle, we don't have to do it ourselves. Christ will help us. He is the One who can and will "set the captive free."

JOHNNY APPLESEED

You probably never heard of John Chapman, but if I were to call him Johnny Appleseed, some of you might recall something about him. He is remembered for doing an unusual thing—something that not everyone else was doing. Johnny Appleseed was a real person, not just a folk hero, and the project he carried out from 1801 to 1834 is still bearing fruit. But he did become a legend, and it's hard to tell how much about his story has been exaggerated.

If you had met him, you probably would have said he was sort of kooky looking. He wore his hair long, which was a bit unusual for a younger man of his day. His only garment was made from a coffee-bean bag. He never wore shoes, and his hat was a tin stew pot. He always carried a burlap bag which contained apple seeds that he had scrounged from the cider mills. While growing up in Massachusetts, he had heard that there were very few fruit trees in the midwestern states. He decided to do something to change that.

We first meet him as he came to Licking Spring, Ohio. Instead of buying a piece of land and settling down to farm it, as most people did, he just found a small space that had no trees and that no one seemed to be using, and he planted it with apple seeds. He then put a fence around the clearing and soon moved on as quietly as he had come. This went on for more than thirty years as he made his way through Ohio, Indiana, and Michigan. Not only did he plant apple seeds in clearings, but also in the fence rows that lined the roads he travelled. Hardly anyone ever knew him as John Chapman. They always referred to him as Johnny Appleseed.

During those years, he started thousands of apple trees that gave shade, nourishment, and refreshment to many people. To him, apples and apple trees were important, and he wanted to share them with the world. People knew and remembered him for the good he did.

The Bible has much to say about our responsibility to share good things with others. It is better to give than to receive. As

Christians, we possess the Word of God, which is food for our souls. But it is also the seed that gives eternal life, and that is the most important seed of all. It is our duty and privilege to plant it in the lives of others—to share it with them. We plant the seed, and God gives the increase. Like Johnny Appleseed, let's try to leave the world better than we found it, not necessarily by planting apple seeds, but by planting seeds of love, kindness, good will, forgiveness, and many other things that bring happiness to people.

Drop a few of those seeds here and there. Some will take root and bear fruit. Then our world will be a much nicer place in which to live.

You, like Johnny Appleseed, can have a vision or dream of what you would like to do in the world. Then do something about making it come true.

BAD COMPANY

"If sinners entice you, do not give in to them" (Proverbs 1:10).

Polly was the pet parrot of a family that lived in the country. She was so tame that she pretty much had the run of the small farm. The tips of her wing feathers had been clipped. Oh, she could still fly, but only for short distances. Like many parrots, she had learned to talk. New words came to her quickly and easily.

The farmer had planted a field of corn, but as soon as the young and tender shoots began to appear above the ground, so did the crows. Every day they landed on the field and ate the tiny plants. The farmer decided that if he was to get a crop of corn, something was going to have to be done about the crows.

One day he shouldered his shotgun and hid behind a rail fence. He watched and waited until several crows had gathered for their morning feast of tender corn plants. Then he made a sudden noise to frighten them into flight. As they took to the air, he fired both barrels of the gun into the flock.

When he walked over to survey the effects of his blast, he discovered three dead crows and one injured parrot struggling on the ground. It seems that Polly had followed him to the field that morning and had begun mingling with the crows without his knowing it. He picked up the injured parrot and discovered one of the pellets in the shot had broken a wing. He took her back to the house, bandaged up the wing, and placed Polly in her cage.

When the children came home after school, they asked, "Who hurt Polly?"

Their father replied, "Bad company." He went on to explain that if Polly had not been in the company of the crows, her wing would not have been broken. Immediately, Polly painfully repeated the words, "Bad company" and kept on repeating them for days after.

Bad company is one of the main reasons people make mistakes and get into trouble. Sometimes we call it peer pressure, and that is one of the strongest influences in the lives of young people. Of course, if your peers are spiritually minded and morally good, such peer pressure can influence you for good. But if your peers are not Christians, and have questionable morals, they don't have anything good to contribute to you. Unless we are absolutely certain and committed to the idea that we can do them more good by our influence than they can do us harm, it's wiser and better to stay out of their company. Bad company will never make us good.

PROCESSIONAL CATERPILLARS

"Do not follow the crowd in doing wrong" (Exodus 23:2).

The Bible says that each one of us is responsible for his own actions. It is never necessary or wise to take up doing anything just because everyone else seems to be doing it. Before we fall in line and follow anyone, it's a good idea to find out where they are going and then decide whether we want to go there.

One day Jean Henri Fabre, a French naturalist, found some processional caterpillars crawling around the rim of a large flower pot. He picked up a few more and placed them so that they made a continuous line, nose to tail around the pot. In such a situation, it would be difficult to tell who is doing the leading. So around and around they went in a complete circle. This went on for a whole week until all of them died of exhaustion or starvation, even though food was nearby, within reach and in plain sight. It was just outside the range of the circle. How foolish it seems to us, but that's the way processional caterpillars operate.

We are not processional caterpillars, even though sometimes we act much as they do. We develop habit patterns; our ways of thinking become firmly established and it is easier and more comfortable to follow them than to cope with change—even when change may prove to be our salvation.

Don't be like a processional caterpillar with your nose glued to your neighbor's back. Do you know where he is leading you? Is he the kind of person who is worthy of being followed? The pressures of friends and playmates are very strong. Do what you know is right, even if you have to do it alone. Wrong is wrong even if everyone else is doing it, and right is right even if no one else is doing it.

On a headstone in a cemetery near Boston, Massachusetts, these words are engraved:

    Look well, my friend and cast your eye;
    As you are now, so once was I.
    As I am now so you must be;
    Prepare for death and follow me.

One day someone stood and read these words and then wrote the following two lines on the stone as his response.
To follow you I'm not content—
Until I know just where you went!
And that's good advice!

WILL WISHING MAKE IT SO?

"Faith without deeds is dead" (James 2:26).

Many years ago there was a popular song with the title, "Wishing Will Make It So." Don't you believe it! Getting things to happen is not all that simple or easy. We know that you don't just make a wish, wave your hand like a wand in the air, repeat some magic words, and expect to see the wish fulfilled right before your eyes.

I have a story to illustrate what I mean. Fred, the gardener, was busy raking up the many leaves that had fallen onto the big lawn surrounding the house. The boy of the family watched as Fred carefully made sure that not one leaf escaped his rake.

"Fred," said the boy, "wouldn't it be great if you could just make a wish and all those leaves would come together in a pile?"

"Oh, I can do that," the gardener replied.

"O.K. Let's see you do it," the boy dared.

"Hear ye, hear ye, all you leaves: get on the pile," Fred ordered as he continued his raking, even more rapidly than before, until every last leaf had been put on the pile.

"See, that's the way you make wishes come true," Fred explained. "You know what you want. Just roll up your sleeves, go ahead, and bring it about."

Boys and girls, in your studies you will learn about many people—scientists, engineers, physicists, doctors, inventors, and all kinds of people who have worked wonders that seemed like magic to bring change, blessing, and improvement to our world. If you remember to look very carefully at each one, you will discover that all of them used the gardener's system. They wished for something to change or happen, or they had a dream, and then they set to work to bring it to pass. That's the only kind of wishing that makes anything happen!

THE LITTLE BOAT TWICE OWNED

Like most other boys his age, Bruce loved boats. He and his playmates spent many hours at a harbor near the little town where they lived, watching boats come and go. It was always an exciting adventure. His home was located on the shore of a large lake, and he often wished he might have a little boat of his own to sail on its waters.

One day his father suggested, "Why don't you make your own boat? I'm sure we can find plenty of materials, and you can use my tools. I will help you." Bruce excitedly accepted the offer.

He and his father spent many happy hours in the shop together as Bruce designed and fashioned his very own little boat. What love and dreams he put into it! He painted it red and blue and made white sails for it. He was proud of it because it was something he had not purchased from a store but had made himself.

He spent many happy hours walking and running on the shores of the lake while his little boat sailed this way and that as it was pushed along by gentle winds, guided and controlled by the long rope Bruce held in his hand. For a while, all went well; then one day as he was sailing his pride and joy, he heard the "Clang, Clang" of the fire alarm in their little town. Quickly he tied the rope to a small twig he had pushed into the sand and hurried off to see the fire. It was a very bad fire. A whole city block lay in ashes and rubble when it was finally put out. Of course, Bruce stayed around watching until all the excitement was over. Finally, his thoughts turned to his little boat. He rushed back to the lake, but, alas, it was nowhere to be seen. For hours he searched, but not a trace of his red, white, and blue boat could be found. Every day he returned to the shore, hoping for a glimpse of his treasure, but he never saw it again.

He grieved so hard about this that one day his father offered to buy him a new boat. But Bruce said, "It wouldn't be like the one I made with my own hands."

After several weeks, a strange thing happened. Bruce and his father were walking together down the main street of their little town when Bruce saw a little boat in a store window.

He shouted excitedly to his father, "Daddy, there's my boat!"

"How do you know it's your boat?" his father asked.

"I know it's mine; don't you see that mark on the front?"

"But there is a price on this boat. It's for sale," his father continued.

Together they entered the store and Bruce walked up to the proprietor and said, "I've come for my boat."

"What do you mean, you've come for your boat? That is not your boat," replied the shopkeeper.

"But I made it with my own hands in my father's shop," Bruce explained. Then he told him how he had lost it on the day of the big fire. The shopkeeper replied that he had purchased it from a fisherman on the evening of the fire.

"Young man," said the shopkeeper, "I'll sell that boat to you for exactly the same price I paid the fisherman for it." And he named the price.

Bruce didn't have to think very long about his decision. He paid for it with his own money. Now the boat that he had made was his again.

Soon after he arrived home, he went to his own room, carrying his redeemed treasure under his arms. His parents could hear him as he said to his toy: "Little boat, you're twice mine now. You were mine in the beginning because I made you. Then I lost you. You are mine again because I bought you. Oh, how I love you!"

His parents thought of another example of the same sort of thing. It was the relationship between us and our Lord and Savior. We are twice His. First we are His by creation; He made us. Then we are His by purchase; we were bought with the precious blood of the Lord Jesus. Like the little boat, a Christian is not his own because he has been "bought at a price" (1 Corinthians 6:20).

A FEATHERED TALE

"Set a guard over my mouth, O Lord; keep watch over the door of my lips" (Psalm 141:3).

The Bible has much to say about gossip and other ways of saying unkind things about one another. These are what we call "sins of the tongue," and they are very wicked in the sight of God. Sometimes we inflict damage to another person with our tongue, damage that can never be undone.

This story has been around a long time. I suppose that no one really knows who told it the first time. The reason it has been around so many years is that the lesson it teaches is as fundamental as the A B C's or the multiplication table. We should learn it early in life and never forget it.

Once upon a time, there was a woman who repeated a bit of gossip about one of her neighbors. It was a juicy morsel, and it grew bigger and bigger as it travelled from tongue to tongue until everyone in her village had heard it. It caused a great deal of sorrow and heartache to the person about whom it was told.

Then one day, the teller of the tale discovered that the story was not true. She was sad as she thought about what she had done. She went to a wise man for advice on how she might repair the damage she had been responsible for.

He listened attentively to her story and then said to her: "Go to the market and purchase a live fowl, large or small; any kind of a fowl will do. Have the butcher kill it for you, but he is not to remove its feathers. On your way home, pull out the feathers as you go and drop them along the way."

She was surprised at this strange bit of advice. She could not understand how his counsel was related to her problem. Anyway, she did what he had asked her to do.

The next day she reported to the wise man that she had done as he had suggested. "Now," said he, "go and gather up all those feathers and bring them to me."

Again she walked the road she had travelled the day before. Soon she discovered that the wind had blown most of the feathers away. She spent the whole day searching, but she found only a handful to bring to the wise man.

"You see," he said, "it was easy to drop the feathers in the first place, but impossible to retrieve them. So it is with gossip and slander. It is easy to make false statements about your neighbor, but it is impossible to right the wrong you have done. Go back to your home now, apologize to the neighbor you harmed, ask for her forgiveness, and after this avoid all gossip."

This truth is good for both young and old. The ninth Commandment tells us not to give false testimony against our neighbor. You cannot be held accountable for words you did not say.

HOW HERCULES KILLED THE MONSTER

In the legends and fables of the Greeks, Hercules was a noble hero. He performed many great and mighty deeds. Most of the statues of him show him carrying his big club. According to one of these fables, he was walking along a very narrow road when he was met by a strange and terrible-looking monster, who was about to attack him. Hercules whacked him on the head with a mighty blow and went on his way thinking he had killed the beast.

How surprised he was when a bit farther down the road he met the same creature again preparing to attack him. This time the monster was three times larger than he was before. Again Hercules began to club the beast—each blow heavier than the one before. It seemed that he should have been beating it to a lifeless pulp, but it just wouldn't lie down and die like any respectable critter would have done. Instead, with each blow, it became bigger and bigger until its mangled body filled up the whole roadway. I'm sure Hercules must have been very discouraged by this time and must have wondered what to do next.

At just that time, Pallas came along and whispered to Hercules, "Leave the beast alone," she said, "for the monster's name is 'Strife'"—which means fighting or quarreling. And would you believe it? He ignored it, and, sure enough, it began to shrivel up until there was hardly anything left. So Hercules left it to die and went on his way.

Of course, this is a myth or a fable, but it teaches us a lesson. If we become involved in a quarrel and begin fighting (striving) with someone, the more we fight, the bigger and worse the whole situation becomes. Of course, just to walk away may not always be the best solution to a quarrel. More often we need to apologize, say we're sorry, and talk the problem out so we understand each other and then forgive and make up. When we handle differences in this way, our world will be much brighter and more peaceful than it was before, and we'll feel a lot better inside.

A very wise man in the Old Testament said, "Without wood, a fire goes out" (Proverbs 26:20). It really does!

USING THE PIECES

Many years ago, according to one story, there lived and worked in Italy a great artist. He was famous for the mosaics that he created. A mosaic is a work of art made up of small pieces of colored glass or stone carefully fitted together and laid on a base of stucco, cement, or metal. *(Provide an illustration, if possible.)* The works he created sold at very high prices.

In his workshop was a poor little boy whose task it was to clean up the floor and keep the room tidy. He was a quiet little fellow and always did his work well. That was about all the artist knew about him.

One day he came to his master and asked timidly, "Please, Master, may I have for my own the bits of glass you throw away?"

"Why, yes, boy," said the artist. "Those small bits are good for nothing. Do as you please with them."

Day by day, the child might have been seen studying the broken pieces found on the floor, putting some to one side and throwing others away. He seemed to love working for his master in the studio and spent much of his time observing how he fashioned his works of art.

After he had been there for several years, the master one day chanced to enter a little-used store room. In looking around, he came upon a piece of work carefully hidden behind the rubbish. He brought it out into the light, and to his surprise found it to be a very excellent piece of work, nearly finished.

"What great artist could have hidden his work in my studio?" he thought to himself.

At that moment, the young servant entered the room. He stopped short on seeing his master. When he saw the work in his hands, his face blushed with embarrassment.

"What is this?" asked the artist. "Tell me what great artist has hidden his masterpiece in my studio?"

"Oh, Master!" faltered the surprised boy. "It is only my poor work. You know you said I might have the broken bits you threw away. For many months I have been working on it at times when there wasn't anything else I needed to be doing in the studio."

Boys and girls, do you catch the hint? Gather up the bits of time and opportunity that are always lying about, and patiently work out your life's mosaic. It could be a masterpiece to the glory of God!

NO MAGIC FAUCETS

Colonel T. E. Lawrence (of Arabia) tells of an experience two Arabs had in the days when most Arabs knew very little about city ways. While on a trip to England, they saw many things that caused their eyes to open wide in amazement, things such as elevators, refrigerators, and street cars. But nothing caught their fancy quite as much as the hot and cold water faucets they found in their hotel room. It was so exciting they almost jumped up and down every time they used them. They had to have a pair of these magic faucets to take home with them so they could have hot and cold water any time they wished out on the desert in their native land.

When they went to the hardware merchant to buy the faucets, they were in for a surprise. The merchant told them that in order to have hot and cold water in a room or a desert tent, one needed more than a pair of faucets. They had to have a source of water, such as a well or spring, holding tanks, a water main to transport it from the source to the faucets, a filtering device, a pumping station, and finally water pipes which had to be installed. Needless to say, they did not take a pair of faucets back to their homeland.

We may smile at this story, but sometimes we are like those Arabs. We want comforts, handy things, pleasures, and a lot of other good things. But we forget about all the things that must be done behind the scenes to make them possible.

Most of you receive a weekly or monthly allowance from your parents. Do you ever think of how hard they had to work in order to have money to give to you? You may envy the child who gets high grades in school, but do you consider the long hours of time and effort that are spent in study? Quite often we hear someone say, "I would like to be a good Christian." Being a good Christian is within the reach of any person who takes Christ as Savior, spends time in Bible study and prayer, becomes a working part of a church, and gives one's self in service to others. In other words, we are talking about a person who wants to have a pure heart, a clean mind, and a useful life in loyalty to our Lord. The good

Christian life is the result of all of these things, like seeds that have been planted in a garden and bring forth good things to eat, or delicious fruit ripening on a tree. The garden and the tree did not "just happen," just as the hot and cold water running from the faucets did not just happen.

If you want good grades, good friends, and a good reputation, remember the "magic faucets." It takes some work to get these things. It won't happen right away. So keep working, and someday you'll probably have what you want.

THE IRRITATED OYSTER

When oysters are irritated in a certain manner, they are made to produce beautiful, lustrous pearls. Scientists have learned just how to do this to make many more pearls than are formed naturally. Pearls that come into being in this scientific manner are called "cultured" pearls. Seventy-five percent of the pearls on the market today are produced in this way.

The Chinese first discovered this technique in the thirteenth century, but Mr. Kokichi Mikimoto of Japan, who was born in 1860, borrowed and improved on the method used by the Chinese.

First of all, young oysters are gathered from the ocean floor by divers. The oyster's shell, or house, is then opened in a way that does not harm the oyster, and a tiny mother of pearl bead or large grain of sand is placed between the kidney and the stomach of the baby oyster. It is then replaced on the ocean floor. There is nothing the oyster can do to dislodge this "foreign body" from his house; he is constantly aware of its presence. He covers it with a layer of nacre, a hard, lustrous, milky mineral—the substance of which pearls are made. After a number of years, the oysters are gathered again and the pearls are harvested. It requires about five years to produce an average-sized pearl; large ones are produced in ten or more years.

These lessons we can learn from the pearl: it is a product of a living thing; it is the result of an injury done to the oyster that produces it; it is the oyster's answer to that injury; and it is the offending object that becomes, through the work of the injured one, a precious and beautiful gem.

What we do with our troubles is important. Troubles and difficulties are part of life. If we let them, they can control and even ruin us. Many people have shown to the world that it is possible to take weakness, pain, disability, handicaps, and inner hurts and use them as centers of beauty and sources of strength. Perhaps God sometimes allows us to have troubles so that our lives will be better and stronger than if everything were always easy and fun!

DON'T SELL YOUR WINGS

Once upon a time, long, long ago, a father skylark and his small son were flying through the air while the father was singing the praises of skylarks. He wanted his son to be proud of the fact that he was a skylark. Skylarks, so he said, can fly higher and sing sweeter than any other bird. The little fellow was very much impressed as he listened to these lessons over and over again every day as he and his father flew together. One day after the bird had grown into his early teens, as we would say, he was flying alone and close to the ground when he heard the tinkle of bells. Being of a curious nature, as most teens are, he came down to earth to see what it was all about. The string of tiny bells were attached to a small cart being pushed by a crafty and cunning old fox, and this was his song:

"Who will buy; who will buy?
I am selling in all weathers,
Fine and fat and juicy worms
In exchange for skylark feathers."

Now there was nothing that skylarks enjoyed more than fat and juicy worms, but they were not easy to get. One had to scratch and dig and work to come up with one now and then, and Junior Skylark was more interested in doing easier things.

So he inquired of the fox, "How many worms do you give for a feather?"

"Two worms for a single wing or tail feather," the fox replied.

"I've got plenty of feathers," said the little bird to himself. "I'll buy a worm or two." So he did. He plucked some feathers and exchanged them for worms, which he gobbled down with glee as he congratulated himself on the fine deal he had made. The next day he did it again, and the day after that for several days. Sometimes it seemed to him that he could not fly as fast or as high as he used to, but he reasoned it was probably just his imagination.

Because he was a teenager, as bird ages go, his parents felt that he needed to learn to fly without too much supervision; so they didn't keep as close a watch over him as they had before. Apparently no one noticed the absence of some feathers.

Then one day he decided to live it up. He looked up the cunning old fox and exchanged five feathers for ten worms. What a grand feast that was! The next day he repeated the deal and the day after that. On the following day, he did it again and then discovered to his horror that he couldn't get off the ground. The sly old fox chased after him and ate him for lunch.

When the skylarks heard about what had happened, they erected a monument to his memory. Forever after that, as parent skylarks are teaching their young the values of life and the art of flying, they take their little ones to the monument in the meadow, which is inscribed with these words:

"In memory of a foolish skylark;

Hush your note each bird that sings;

In memory of a poor, lost skylark

Who for earthworms sold his wings."

As children and young people grow up, they will be tempted to sell their morals for drugs, alcohol, cigarettes, bad company, and a great many other things. We must remember that the road to success is a very narrow and disciplined road. Keep all the feathers you have. You will need them. Without feathers, a bird cannot fly.

THE IMPORTANCE OF LITTLE THINGS

"For who despises the day of small things?" (Zechariah 4:10).

Do you know what a blacksmith is? A blacksmith is a person who works with iron, making or repairing iron utensils, tools, and horseshoes. There are not very many of them around today, but there are a few. Perhaps you will see one someday.

Fred lived in a small city located on a bay, or inlet of the sea. Its harbor was visited by ships from many parts of the world. As he walked to and from school each day, he passed a blacksmith shop. Many times on his way home, he would stop and watch the smith work at his forge, a large open furnace for heating iron. He enjoyed seeing the sparks fly from the forge as the smith pumped more air into the forge with the bellows. When it got hot enough, he pulled the white-hot iron out of the fire and began to hammer it into shape on the anvil, and the sparks exploded in all directions. Fred noticed how particular the man was in his work. After hammering a piece of iron for a while, he would hold it up, look at it from all sides very carefully, and then thrust it back into the fire.

At one time the blacksmith was engaged in a special and very long-lasting job. He would work on it whenever other tasks were not pressing him. This job went on for many months. He was forging and welding links of a very heavy and long chain. It was to be an anchor chain for one of the ships that often visited the harbor. He seemed to spend so much time hammering and heating and heating and hammering again on the same link. It looked all right to Fred, but it did not satisfy the craftsman; so back again it went to the forge and the anvil until it was just what he wanted it to be.

One day Fred asked him, "Why do you do it so often? Don't you ever get tired of it all, one link after another, and every one looking very much like the one before it?"

"Of course I get tired," the blacksmith replied, "but I want each link to be welded as perfectly as I can weld it. If there is just one weak link in the chain, it will break under strain, no matter how strong the other links are, and maybe a ship will be lost and many people will die. I want the chain to hold." Fred didn't understand all that the answer meant, but he thought of it very often.

After many months the chain was finished. The captain who had ordered it came to inspect it. He was very pleased with it; so he bought it and put it aboard his ship.

Some months later, as the vessel was nearing its home port in a distant land, it was overtaken by a terrible storm in the middle of the night. The ship was being driven helplessly toward the dangerous rocks that lined the shore. The sailors could hear the roar of the waves as they crashed against the rocks. The captain gave the order to drop the anchor—hoping to stop the ship and ride out the storm.

As soon as the anchor caught on a rock on the bottom of the sea, the chain tightened with a jerk. Instantly a link broke, and the vessel continued to drift toward shore. Another anchor was dropped, but the same thing happened.

Finally, the captain gave the order, "Throw out the last anchor; if this one won't hold, we're lost." This last anchor was the one that was on the chain the blacksmith had finished just a few months before. It was thrown overboard; the sailors held their breath in suspense as it disappeared beneath the angry waves. Finally it hit bottom, dragged a few yards and then caught hard on a solid rock. As the chain suddenly tightened, it jerked the ship around almost as though it were trying to tear the bow off the boat. But the chain held! The ship, its crew, and its cargo were all saved. The storm had met its master because a blacksmith had felt that little things were important and valuable. All the little details of welding may not have seemed important to Fred, but they were very important to the ship and its captain and crew that night.

If ever you are tempted to feel that small things are not important, remember that life often depends on small things. Just one weak link in your character could mean disaster and failure.

CHOCOLATE CAKE

The sound of an egg beater drew little Tommy into the kitchen one day, and there he found his mother at work. Her face was rosy except for a dab of flour on one cheek, and she made a pretty picture. For a moment, he looked at her; then he began to watch what she was doing. He would find out just what she put into that chocolate cake that made it so good.

There was chocolate, of course, and Tommy reached for a crumb that had broken off the bar. To his surprise, he found it was bitter. His mother explained that bitter chocolate was used for cooking and baking. Tommy glanced at the other things on the table. There was a cupful of sour milk; surely Mother was not going to put that into the cake! But she did, along with some of that awful baking soda that she had given Tommy once for a stomachache. What kind of cake could she possibly make out of such things as these? Tommy turned up his nose, but his mother only smiled and told him to wait and see.

That evening, Tommy's family was eating dinner when Mother brought out the cake. It looked as good as usual, but Tommy tasted it carefully: a little crumb, then a larger crumb, and finally a whole bite. It couldn't have been better! Tommy forgot about the sour milk and asked for another piece.

Life is not all sweetness. There is much that is bitter, and we hardly see how anything good will come from it. Certainly, all things are not good in themselves, but "all things work together for good" (Romans 8:28, KJV). This is God's promise to them who love Him. Day by day He is making you what He wants you to be, and He will never put anything into your life by mistake. Someday you will see and understand that He knows best.

GOOD WORK PAYS OFF

Scripture Text: 1 Corinthians 3:10-14

A wealthy man had purchased a lovely little home by the side of the sea. Everything about the place was just what he had been looking for except the fence surrounding the property. It was in bad repair and leaned dangerously toward the ocean.

"All I need is to have the fence repaired," he said to himself. "Then what pleasant times I shall spend here."

He inquired among the neighbors about where he might find a good carpenter to do the job. He was told by many that there was a Mr. James who always had plenty of work building and repairing things for the people of the village. They assured him that he would do a good job.

After the rich man had found him and he had come to look over the task, the new owner said, "Just fix it up. Mend it where the need is greatest; put in as many new posts as necessary, but don't spend too much time on it because I will be planting heavy vines that will soon cover it."

After carefully examining the fence and considering the amount of materials and time that would be necessary, Mr. James agreed to repair the fence for fifty dollars.

After the job was completed, the fence was strong and straight at every point. When the owner returned to inspect the work, he remarked, "It looks almost as good as new; you remember, I only asked you to repair it."

"It is as good as new," Mr. James replied.

"But why were you so careful? I told you I was going to cover it with vines," the owner inquired.

Mr. James smiled as he replied, "It doesn't matter how much you cover it with vines. Every time I would pass it in the future, I would feel that I had cheated you if I felt I could have built a better fence. I wanted it to be my best workmanship. I did the best I knew how."

The rich man nodded. "You are right; now how much do I owe you?"

"Just the fifty dollars we agreed upon," answered the workman.

"Great! Here is the fifty dollars for repairing the fence, plus another ten dollars for the principle you built into it." And the owner handed him the money.

Several months passed, and then one day a bad storm beat upon the New England coast where the cottage stood. Almost everything in the area was demolished. But the fence that Mr. James had built stood straight and strong.

Several years later, the people of the village were making plans to erect a city park. Serving on the committee that was planning the park was the wealthy man whose fence Mr. James had rebuilt. Many prospective builders had submitted bids for the construction, but none was entirely satisfactory. Finally, the wealthy man said, "I believe I know the right man for the job. I can assure you that if he does it, it will be done well, and probably better than most others would do it."

Mr. James was contacted, and within a few more months, the park was completed. Everyone was delighted with the fine workmanship he had put into it.

We need to think about the structures we are building every day, the kind of principles we build into our lives. Will they stand the storms and stresses that will beat against them? The quick and easy way is usually not the right or the best way. The kind of material and workmanship that we build into our lives will determine how strong we will be against the strains and stresses that we are sure to meet in the future.

The apostle Paul had this in mind when he wrote his first letter to the Christians in Corinth, in which he said, "Each one should be careful how he builds.... His work will be shown for what it is.... If what he has built survives, he will receive his reward" (1 Corinthians 3:10-14).

More Books For Use With
CHILDREN

God's Wonderful World: 26 Lessons for Primary Church. Here are six months' worth of lessons for leading children of grades 1-3 in meaningful worship. Carolyn Lehman's love for kids and her keen creativity have made this a delightful way to help children see God's love and power in nature. Teacher's book, **#3316;** student activity books, **#3317** and **3318.**

Fun Stuff for Kids, by Norma McPhee. Here is a wide variety of stories and activities for kids 8-12 years old: puzzles, crafts, games, poems, prayers and party ideas. Use them in church or at home. Teacher's book, **#3227;** student activity books, **#3228** and **3229.**

Handbook of Creativity, by Judy Dorsett. No matter what age you work with, here's a book that will help you be more creative. This book will help you implement various teaching methods as well as puzzles, music, drama, puppets, and creative writing to enhance the learning process. **#3226.**

Available at your Christian bookstore or